Somerset

Also by Daniel Donaghy

Start with the Trouble (University of Arkansas Press, 2009)

Streetfighting (BkMk Press, 2005)

Somerset

Daniel Donaghy

NYQ Books™

The New York Quarterly Foundation, Inc.
New York, New York

NYQ Books™ is an imprint of The New York Quarterly Foundation, Inc.

The New York Quarterly Foundation, Inc.
P. O. Box 2015
Old Chelsea Station
New York, NY 10113

www.nyq.org

First Edition

Set in New Baskerville

Layout by Raymond P. Hammond

Cover Design by Raymond P. Hammond

Cover Art: *Hope*, 1886, George Frederic Watts (1817-1904)
(Please note that this painting has been augmented from the original with permission. It has been slightly trimmed on the left side and top to make room for the titling.)

Cover Photograph ©Tate, London 2018

Author Photo by Abigail Donaghy

Library of Congress Control Number: 2018935431

ISBN: 978-1-63045-057-1

For Karen, Abigail, and Eliza

Acknowledgments

Antioch Review: "Somerset"

Blast Furnace: "Poem Ending with a Union Vote," "Philly Still Life: Lehigh Avenue," "What I Did While Wayne Called the Cops"

Cutthroat: "Teaching My Daughter to Ride Her Bike, I Recall the One My Father Stole for Me from a Black Child" (Joy Harjo Poetry Award, Honorable Mention)

december: "Making Shepherd's Pie on St. Patty's Day While My Neighbors Have Make-Up Sex," "Pat McCarthy's Quick Hands," "The Roaches and the Nuns"

Fourteen Hills: "Hood Ghazal"

Free State Review: "Girl On a Playground Swing," "An Old Man Shooting Free Throws," "*What's Up?*"

Hanging Loose: "Elegy for My Mother"

Measure: "The Stroll"

Newfound: "Okay"

New Letters: "Third Month"

Nimrod: "Bike Ride" and "Wren on Osage"

North American Review: "Boys Find Two Babies in Palethorp Street Weeds"

Notre Dame Review: "Pigeon Man, Grafton Street" and "What Cement Is Made Of"

Poet Lore: "Puzzle"

Paterson Literary Review: "The Background Noise I've Heard All My Life," "Between Better Days," "Birthday Poem for My Mother," "Greg's Poem," "In Praise of Lying Flat on My Back," "My Aunt Edna Gives Me a Postcard Photo," "Our Block's First Black Couple," "Testament"

Seneca Review: "Vanishing" (under another title)

Slipstream: "Needle Park" (as "McPherson Square")

Southern Humanities Review: "Ice Skating with My Daughter"

Sou'wester: "Empty"

Stone Canoe: "Bank Day"
SPECS: "90°"
Tar River Poetry: "Peace"
Tusculum Review: "Nothing, October"

I would also like to thank Maria Mazziotti Gillan, Harry Humes, John Bargowski, and especially Steve Myers for the careful attention they gave these poems. Thanks to Christopher Torockio and Ed Case for their years of friendship and support.

CONTENTS

Philly Still Life: Lehigh Avenue

At two in the morning, when the moon
        has clacked off with the El,

trailing sparks from a dying star
        along the steel horizon,

dome light leaks through tinted windows
        thumping at intersections,

neon blares from the corner bar,
        a TV flickers in a drafty apartment,

where a mother sits like an empty lot
        at a cracked glass table,

twirling the ember of her smoke in ash.

Needle Park

McPherson Square Park, in the Kensington section of Philadelphia, houses a domed, classically-designed branch of the city's library. It is known locally as "Needle Park" because of the syringes that drug users discard there daily.

after Jeffrey Stockbridge's photograph "Jamie"

I'm going to turn into a pillar tonight
atop the library steps in Needle Park.

I'm going to stand beside the young addict
whose pregnant belly domes a green T-shirt,
whose hard stare granites the dark,

going to listen to the song of the street:
a boy charming blues from a bucket,
the staccato tapping of a car date's honk.

When she slides from a front seat
to snort or shoot or grab a quart,
then falls back to us, shoe soles blank

as skulls, I'm going to trace her tracks past
these alleys and rolling gates, these piles of shit,
past charred cars and the bricked bank

and glass shards calling for your wrist.
I'm going to lean in to pick up the static

of her synapses while over us El trains clack
and night rejects the few stars' offer of light.

Somerset

It is summer-gone that I see, it is summer-gone.
The sweet flowers indrying and dying down,
The grasses forgetting their blaze and consenting to brown.
—Gwendolyn Brooks, "A Sunset of the City"

An El train squeals into Somerset like it
doesn't want to stop, like it knows what is

wilting in its shadows—summer-gone
corner boys, women tricking in bars that
peddle *rock* and *dope*, *weed* and *wet* to guys I

might have known as a child. Somerset, see,
is Zombieland: abandominiums, speedballs to the neck. It

is storefront ministries, pawnshops, no cops. Is
a father's fist, a daughter's scream. Is summer-gone
as the smokestacks and textile mills that spilled the

street's first darkness. Gone as a huckster's sweet
corn, as a widow's flowers

flaming in a window box, as a junkie indrying
in a burned-out car, lost to meth mouth and
swallowed by chest-high weeds. The El knows dying,

knows when to shut its doors. Down
on Somerset, they're dispensing free samples of the

day's best. They're kneeling in alley grasses
denying their sponsors, forgetting
the missionaries who nodded all morning through their

heartbreak and new-start promises. Blaze.
Spoon sizzle. Time screeches still as an El train and

they curl up in God's blanket, consenting
to a ride that will get them only back to
Somerset and their next round of brown.

13

Our Block's First Black Couple

Before our family fell into Philly
when we lost the Levittown house,
before I snapped my ankle
when I failed to fly
from an abandoned rooftop
onto used mattresses,
before I watched a suicide's blood
drip from an El train's wheel
onto my screaming sister's head,
fathers of my future friends
nodded over slotted ashtrays
in track-shadowed Tinney's Bar
exactly how and when
and then, one July night,
no one in the neighborhood
heard or saw anything—not
the basement window's smash,
not the flock of fat men
running down Albert Street
to a car to the bar to the beers
they'd been sipping
all evening, officer, while
our block's first black couple
slept through flames.

The Stroll

a nickname locals gave Kensington Avenue,
which sits beneath the Market-Frankford El in Philadelphia

Get clean or get killed: the motto of The Stroll.
She works in parked cars, alleyways, and lots
around the block from where she went to school.
Clacking El train sparks orange the night.

Between a car, an alley, and a vacant lot,
she'd choose the car: a door handle to open.
El trains clack and spark, El tracks bring night.
Walking dates are the most dangerous—

she could scream from a car, a door might open.
Plus, a walker has no license plate:
she and her friends share lists of the most dangerous.
The Strangler was a walking date: light-skinned,

closely cropped hair, goatee, no license plate
to track him through the wilderness of weeds
in which he choked three women. He left skin,
though, that whispered beneath their fingernails,

that tracked him through the wilderness of weeds
down muddy paths of condoms, beer cans, needles.
Though he left skin under their fingernails,
The Strangler says he didn't mean to kill.

Down muddy paths of condoms, beer cans, needles,
she is beaten, raped, or robbed most nights she tricks.
The Strangler says he didn't mean to kill.
The El lamplights are no match for the dark.

She's been beaten, raped, and robbed, but still she tricks
around the block from where she went to school.
The El lamplights are no match for the dark.
Get clean or get killed: the motto of The Stroll.

What's Left of Osage
West Philadelphia, 2017

First glance tells you something's wrong:
        there should be elbows

on these railings, lace curtains breathing
        in this blue morning's breeze,

should be brake lights, turn signals,
        rising and falling bass,

should be kids dribbling toward hoops,
        Mingus wafting

from back kitchens, parking spots
        saved with folding chairs.

But this is what's left of Osage Avenue,
        thirty-two years after police

bombed house 6221, bombed MOVE
        and its garbage heaps,

its rants against *the system,*
        since they let a neighborhood burn.

It was the day after Mother's Day.
        On front stoops across the city,

our parents flicked ashes
        and shook their heads.

Our fathers kept saying
        niggers and *nigger neighborhood,*

look at those animals, until we said it, too.
        There's no trace

in today's spring sky
of the 10,000 rounds

of police bullets, of fire hoses blasting
MOVE's rooftop bunker

from cranes, no hovering chopper
about to drop C-4,

no billowing smoke, no flames,
no firemen watching those flames

spill from house to house
until the whole block blazed,

no sirens or screams from the corner
that there were children in that house.

I stand where a reporter did,
jacket off, tie undone

in the heat. I hear again his search
for words, see his head turned

to the burning houses, to where police shot
at Ramona Africa, unarmed,

and Birdy Africa, a naked child,
as they fled the fire,

to where the Medical Examiner's van
would idle days later, heavy

with eleven MOVE bodies, five of them children,
to where the mayor would break

ground that July, smiling in his hardhat
      beside the displaced in their hardhats,

promising *to make them whole again.*
      Here's what he made them:

roofs that can't keep out the rain,
      beams that can't hold the floors,

burst pipes, flooded basements,
      cedar siding a funnel for the cold.

He made a ghost town when he offered
      to buy back, for pennies on the dollar,

houses he'd immediately condemn
      and half the block left.

Close your eyes. Hear moving
      vans beeping in reverse,

hear those who stayed whispering
      behind screen doors

and upstairs curtains,
      across evening tables trying

to figure how much would be enough
      to start over, and where,

hear them crying because they're too old
      to start over,

hear them trying to figure who'd move next,
      hear them praying,

hear them slamming fists on those tables
       and into plastered walls

they know would quickly turn to ash
       because they should not

have to move, because *the city,*
       by God, needs to make this right.

Next, hear silence falling flat
       as awning shadows

over Osage, where in every
       boarded window a nail gun

still rings rifle-loud, where today
       nothing moves

except a scrawny wren that hunts bugs
       on the heaved sidewalk,

flits a moment in a budding maple—
       our fathers kept saying *niggers*

and *nigger neighborhood*
       look at those animals,

until we said it, too—
       then disappears.

Boys Find Two Babies in Palethorp Street Weeds

Let the boys not find what they found.
Let them take 2nd Street
to the pizza shop on Berks

rather than cutting down Palethorp,
more alley than street,
as anyone around here knows.

Every house bulldozed.
Sidewalks overtaken by weeds
taller than the used car lot's fence.

The empty lot's cinderblock wall.
Tall enough to swallow a sofa.
A car fender. Paint cans. Boards.

Ripped bags of garbage and clothes.
To hide for weeks two babies
who lived maybe an hour.

Whom the boys thought were dolls.
Medical specimens, police said.
Umbilical cords still attached.

Let the boys go on thinking
they're dolls. Let them be dolls.
Naked, wide-eyed baby dolls.

Faces blue and cut open.
Stomachs cut open.
Reeking of formaldehyde.

A boy and a girl.
One big, one small.
Hard to say if they're twins.

Let the boys go on dribbling
behind their backs,
between their legs until

thin crust folds in their hands.
Let them go on.
Money tucked into soaked socks.

Ball echo the street's sound.
Let the boys go on being 9 and 12.
Let them not find what they found.

After Hearing the Pedophile Died

I don't know if I was the only boy
he asked to carry boxes up his stairs,
if he chilled all his root beer mugs

or just the one he handed to me,
twelve or thirteen, my father gone,
my mother laughing with him

on his stoop before she said
Sure, he'll help you, Joe.
Send him home when you're done.

Before he closed his door,
pointed to boxes in the dark hall,
said *Thanks, I owe you,* then

started up the stairs, one at a time,
in no rush, curtains drawn,
the only light his bedroom lamp.

I don't know why I didn't
make an excuse and leave,
why I've never told anyone.

I didn't know *pedophile* then,
only *stranger danger*—
but Joe was no stranger,

just strange, we all thought,
lonely and sad, harmless—
and *child molester,*

but he didn't molest me,
really, just led me
to the foot of his bed

where a reel-to-reel film
flickered on a screen,
black-and-white, no sound

except the grinding projector,
two men, a woman
going back and forth

between them with her mouth
while they kissed each other.
Joe said he was the one on the left.

How good she felt.
Wouldn't I like that?
He could do it to me right now.

He said he wasn't joking.
Then he said he was.
We're just two guys talking, right?

he said. *Just shooting the shit.*
Now don't you go lying....
I don't know what I was thinking

when he left and came back
with a root beer float
or why I stared at the screen

while younger Joe and his friends
changed positions,
while older Joe, *Loner Joe,*

we called him, lay on his bed
touching himself
until I turned around.

I didn't know about the deadbolt,
so his front door didn't open
before he wanted it to

to the sun's white glare
off a moving truck, to salsa
blaring from a Subaru,

drowning out whatever
Joe whispered before I raced
that car all the way home.

Empty

after Jeffrey Stockbridge's photograph "Tic Tac and Tootsie"

No such thing as an empty house.
Pull out the copper pipes,
smash all the windows, gut the place,

and still nursery pink will tint white
hallway walls, wood floors will read
dog scratch and *chair scrape*

in a language of scars.
Take this photo: twin sisters
on a row home stoop, eyes shadow-

lost, slouching knee-to-knee before
a doorframe's sheet of plywood.
Home is where your clothes are,

and theirs lie behind them
in a black trash bag, beneath
bricks painted blue on one side

of the door, brown on the other.
Imagine someone's bright idea
of marrying mud with the sea.

Imagine what neighbors might
have thought on their way back
to their own cramped castles—

nothing to write anyone about,
but home nonetheless.
No such thing as empty eyes,

whether they're staring
you down, like the sister's
seven minutes older,

or lost in their own clouds,
like the younger one's, whose arms
hang like a marionette's cut free.

These girls are maybe twenty:
spaghetti straps and short skirts,
hair pulled tight into pony tails

pink as poodles. Whatever
will save or kill them waits
somewhere out of frame.

No such thing as an empty house.
Promises groove the threshold
of every clicked-shut door.

What Cement Is Made of

The cement plant—where all day wind spirals
aggregate around scaffolds and storage
bins tall as steeples—has only three walls,

so it opens to Route 1 like a stage.
Five o'clock: dump trucks and conveyer belts
stiffen like workers on washroom stools

who stare into their brown or black hands,
or who close their eyes, savoring already
that first lager's cold burn against their throats.

Inside locker doors: pictures of wives, kids,
strippers, stenciled numbers. Crusted cement
on toilet tanks, across the line of sinks.

In shower stalls, concrete mix washes off
like limestone loosened by hard summer rain
under a single, shared fluorescent bulb.

The young supervisor slips off waders
and safety goggles and dreams of softballs
arcing toward the rusted steel of the sun.

Diesel and dust turn to soap and cologne,
the day's heavy falling to rap music,
phone calls, texts, doors opening and closing.

Tomorrow's flatbeds glare from loading docks.
Sea gulls stalk the drum-gray air overhead.
Men ease their wasting bodies into jeans,

T-shirts, ball caps. They wait for each other
to pull on clean socks, lace their boots, then rise
together, laughing, toward their evenings.

Elegy for My Mother

She liked most couches in sunny rooms,
game shows and soap operas, her dog,
glasses of iced tea sweating on end tables

like candles at a dinner party, or else
calls with news she could tell and retell,
hours on the front stoop watching life

keep happening to everyone but herself.
It should not have surprised us, then,
when she kept silent and hoped

what was wrong would go away.
Or when she became the good patient,
early for appointments, taking her pills

and keeping to her diet, sleeping
in the cleansing chair each Monday,
Wednesday, and Friday morning while

the machine filtered her blood.
Or when she made all of the final plans,
left the paperwork like love letters

on her dresser, which we found after
she couldn't talk or even breathe
without the other machine that sat

over her right shoulder, that she, on one
good day, didn't need, and could say
she loved us and they could turn it off,

so they did.

Hood Ghazal

Philadelphia, PA

In the '90s, slumlords swirled like smoke over Kensington,
snatched up the empty row houses in Kensington,

cut them into apartments for transients, offered no heat,
leaking roofs, creeping mold throughout Kensington,

brought alleys clogged with diapers, syringes, rotten meat,
brought crack dealers, squatters, prostitutes to Kensington,

scoured the obits, brought nasturtiums, flowering cat's feet
to grieving widows looking to move quickly from Kensington,

let those houses crumble, bought out neighbors to complete
the transmogrification of entire blocks of Kensington,

left graffiti, junkies, burned-out cars in the streets,
left boarded windows, shuttered stores across Kensington,

which once held block-long textile mills, each with its fleet
of waiting trucks, each with gangs of workers from Kensington,

where once in parlors pianos danced, where once girls beat
on porches rugs their brothers lost fingers making in Kensington.

Between Better Days

On warm childhood afternoons
I'd stalk head-high weeds

beside Tinney's Bar for anything
I could snatch with a cupped hand—

crickets, grasshoppers,
now and then a praying mantis

chomping on a fly—and clink
into my jar, where they'd hop

and spit what we called tobacco
on sticks and grass I'd tossed in there,

as if they'd live for long
cramped like that on a shelf

in the cramped bedroom
I shared with my parents

after we lost our second house
and set up in an apartment

my uncle owned, where I slept
between the foot of their bed

and the console TV/radio/record player
they'd bought in better days,

my cot easy to fold up each morning
and push to the wall, my nose cold

against the thin glass between me
and those ready eyes and legs

and frightening mouths,
still as I was those moments

before I took that jar with me
on my walk to school past worn

women working Kensington Ave.
even that early, past huffers

huddled outside the lumber yard's
barbed-wire gates hoping for day work,

beneath the clacking, sparking El,
opening the jar as I passed that lot,

waiting for the bugs to vanish long before
I'd figure out how to disappear myself.

Puzzle

My father and I piece together
a puzzle at the oval glass table.
For twelve hours today
he wired boats, scaled masts,
breathed in God knows what

from gutted submarine walls.
Tonight, a Pall Mall smokes
in his ashtray, a Schaefer can
sweats in nicotined light
while he teaches me

to start with the frame—
hay and grass floor,
sides of sawmill and sheep,
cloudless blue sky
crowded by a silo, willows,

crows on a wood-shingled roof—
his breaths long and slow
before he drives off and leaves
us with the puzzle our lives
would become—welfare,

food stamps, government cheese,
so much whispering to collectors
on our front stoop, so much talk
of losing our house, our lights,
our heat, of there being

nowhere else in the world
for us to go beyond our water-
buckled ceiling and rotting floors,
beyond our always-damp dirt cellar
that washed out our old photos,

where our pants and shirts hang-
dry in winter until they're stiff
as the cardboard pieces
my father and I snap into place
for a good hour together,

his arm around my shoulder,
our hands a single machine
that patches together a barn door,
a tractor, a white picket fence
before we step back in that

for-once quiet kitchen, smiling,
him whistling as the refrigerator
kicks on, to marvel at what
we've done, to enter for a moment
a world so perfectly assembled

that all its edges disappear.

90°

for Bud Fisher

First job, first day: I'm with Javier
bottling nail polish remover

in a beauty supply factory.
Javier needs to pee, but won't go.

It feels like I'm bleeding flames, he says.
On break, he asks me if I want to

get high, if I can front him ten bucks
until payday. Javier's my boss.

I'm sixteen. Never had a payday
or the clap. Javier's married. He's

afraid he spread the flames to his wife.
Around us, rusted, windowless walls

cough forklift exhaust and peroxide,
cough bleach, acetone, silk screener's ink.

I scored the job through a ministry
aimed at helping kids out of the hood,

at getting us work experience
so we knew why we should stay in school.

My friend Bud's here, too, making boxes.
At lunch he'll school Javier in hoops

and get fired for it. *Bud* as in
Budweiser, his dad's beer, white cans

that Javier and Darrell knock back
before they light up a blunt. Darrell

handles the forklift and loads boxes
all day into the empty bellies

of trucks he never sees the fronts of.
I never see him without headphones

to block out sound or funnel it in.
Before Javier hires Bud back,

he calls Bud's mom a parade of names.
Before we started, that ministry

put Bud and me and a bunch of kids
through an interview class: how to dress,

how to bend our elbows exactly
ninety degrees before we shook hands.

No less or you'll look needy, the guy
said. *Any more is too far away.*

What a bunch of bullshit, I can hear
Javier telling that guy. *Go ask*

your mother how her angle's doing.
Or better yet, go ask Bud's mother.

Watch out: she set my junk on fire.
All summer Bud and I groan and sweat

and fill boxes for minimum wage.
We answer when Javier's wife calls

and say he's on a delivery
when he's really out back with his girl.

We learn a bunch about measurements
that summer—pallet capacity,

truck volume—learn that Javier's wife
can run a sub-6-minute mile

and that Javier's only real marriage
is to lies. We start seeing ninety

degrees everywhere—forklift to truck,
punch card to time clock, 55-gallon

drum to the always-slick shop floor—
how just a few degrees either way

and any curious spark would mean
all of us bleeding serious flames.

What I Did While Wayne Called the Cops

Because his hands were cuffed
behind his back, because I was 16,
because the tongues of his lace-
less boots were curled and dry,
because he was older than my father
and bug-eyed high, reeking
of piss, crying through snot
that no one would bail him out,
because I'd been raised to fear
black people, because
he'd called me *sir*, because
he'd stolen only Rite-Aid
batteries, because he weighed
so much he had to spread
his legs to make room
for his belly on that plastic
break room chair, because
he kept saying *It's not fair,
not fair*, I couldn't chase
him when he ran, grunting,
for the door, before the jeans
belted across his thighs
tripped him like our rent-a-cop's
blackjack, before his open
mouth bounced on the floor.

Pat McCarthy's Quick Hands

for P.M., wherever you are

Thirty years ago today,
        off from sixth grade
so the nuns could tell
            our parents our sins,

my friends and I set out
        to rob or ride box cars
along the P&R line,
            but found instead

an old coaling station
        we almost couldn't
break into. We thought
            it was a warehouse,

didn't know about
        the chutes in the floor,
and when I stepped into
            the dark mouth of one

I was gone without fear
        or a fight and would never
have known I left this life
            after a forty-foot fall

into steel dividers
        that did their work on me.
Only a year with a shrink
            brings it back:

Brian sidestepped the lip
        and I kept going
with Pat McCarthy behind me
            in shit-kicker boots

and black gloves, twirling
       his homemade blackjack.
Big Pat, our hockey team's
          tough guy,

twice my size and therefore
       able to snatch my wrist
and keep me here,
         swing me

toward the chute wall
       that smashed my face,
toward all the days between
         that one and today,

when I'm in our living room
       thinking of Pat
and whatever he became,
         thinking I'd call

my mother if she were alive,
       then turning to watch
a bluebird, fat from our feeders,
         flit on our deck railing

just beyond this window,
       my daughters in school,
my wife at work,
         my work these words

I find between reading poems
       and sipping coffee,
easy, so far today from the fights
         back there,

and the deaths,
        the nights sleeping
with my own blackjack in my bed,
            just in case,

squeezing it when car horns blared
        or bottles smashed,
staring this March morning
            of thaw and gray

into my palms, calling back
        Pat looking up
only at the instant he had to
            to see

the drop coming before I did,
        and next thing I know
I'm hanging again in Pat's
            quick hands,

eye socket broken, forehead
        slashed, feet held up
by nothing as they kick the air.
            I'm crying

while Pat's lifting me out
        of the hole, screaming
I got you, man, I got you,
            and he does.

Bank Day

One Saturday morning a month
        my mother and I strolled
Kensington Avenue to the bank—

strolled the way you could
        that shadowed street then,
our shoulders almost touching,

my passbook and envelope
        of found change clicked
into her purse while the El clattered

overhead and shops raised their gates
        to the day, Dennery's Sports
wheeling out racks of shorts and shirts

on sale, Phil's Appliances lining
        the curb with used stoves.
Then the pool hall's dark, Kellis Bar's

neon glow, the Laudromat's
        early rumble and hum,
the refrigerated cold of Hymie's Deli

pouring out its doors and over us
        as we passed its stacks
of the *Bulletin* and *Daily News*

and hungry third shifters waiting
        on hoagies and cheese fries
at Bill's Steaks' take-out window.

I was thirteen. It was almost a year
        since my father drove off.
My mother could have used

that change, no doubt, but
        never said so
during our two-mile walks

or any time before or after,
        her perm Aqua Netted
into place, no sign

in her husky-blue eyes
        that my father's checks
every other week weren't enough

and that she'd signed up
        for food stamps,
no sign of anything wrong at all

as she smiled at bargains
        in the storefront windows
of Levin's Furniture and Kresge's

Five and Dime, as she pulled me
        inside Humphries Drugs
for samples of their homemade sweets—

fudge, nonpareils, salted pecans,
        sticky salt water taffy,
dipped strawberries and raisins

and crunchy malt balls melting
        in our hands and our mouths,
leaving a rim of chocolate

around our lips that we'd slyly
        lick away as we stepped
back into slatted light

and continued on, past lost love
        crying from The Record Spot,
past Four Sons Pizza, where

soon floured dough would fly
        round as manhole covers
and our wax water cups

would sweat inside our fingers
        when we stopped
for an early lunch and a slice

of the best Sicilian around,
        crust thicker than our thumbs,
mounds of mozzarella drowned

in red sauce rich with garlic
        and chopped basil,
topped with a pinch of pecorino.

First, though, we had to cross
        Allegheny's five-way
spider web, had to climb the stained

marble steps beneath the old clock
        that tolled every hour
back when the block was thick

with mills, factories, and trolley traffic,
        that sat silent above us
while I waited in a winding line

after I'd raised the black pen
        on its beaded chain
and written my account number

and my name, after I'd counted
   that change and my mother
double-checked it, then took

a seat beside a fake fern under
   a big, arched window,
crossing her blue-veined calves,

waving at me to go on
   like she would again
at the end of her life, so I went on,

went up to the handsome man
   who offered a lollypop
I thought myself too old for,

who fed my coins into a counter
   and marked my book
in purple ink, pointing out pennies

of interest I'd made since last time,
   saying *Keep up the good work*
loud enough for my mother to hear.

What's up?

is what Coach on his porch shouts
        into the shouts of two white boys
running at him with their hands

up   out   pumping at their sides
        before what's up goes down:
brake screech   horn blast

high beams sharp as spotlights
        blazing this dazed street's stage.
All the world's a cage here in Kensington

a sprung trap   broken back
        punch line of a neighborhood
where Coach shouts again

into bass and bats
        into black and brown faces
here to make someone prey.

What's up? he shouts
        to the pipe slamming his temple.
What's up? he shouts

pushing shut the door
        they'll kick on top of him.
They will not stop with him

with smashing in his windows
        trashing his laptop
with lamp crash and vase drop.

They want the white boys
        who pushed the black kid
off his bike   want the white

45

boys   white boys.
          White noise most nights:
sirens silent tonight

until the slush-snow
          blinks *redblueredblue*
and neighbors peer

out at the show.
          We know where you live
pipe and pistol whisper

to Coach before they run.
          We know where you live
bat says to Coach's throat.

White boys   Coach's kids
          hall closet with his wife
his life this house this street

this trussed trashed door
          these cops saying *get a gun*
or move these cops saying

if you shoot one outside drag him in
          before you call
saying *pull yourself together*

hey we know it's not right
          saying when they leave
try to have yourself a good night.

Peace

In June's dew-wet sunrise,
he'd park that year's used car—

Dodge Dart with no reverse?
Stingray with the cracked block?—

beside a tidal creek
and pull from the trunk his

crab pot and gloves; the eel,
slimy in wax paper,

that he'd chop for bait; the
small red cooler of Schmidt's

and pretzels that he'd keep
close to him those slow hours

I clawed sand for mole crabs,
chased gulls along the shore,

out of his sight before
sun topped the two-lane bridge

that brought us into town.
Ah, what does he want so

long past his death, coming
back just to turn again

toward the marshy inlet
those purple-pink Jersey

mornings I'd call to him
and he wouldn't answer

so I'd call out again
until at last he'd shout

Come on, pal, will you give
me ten minutes of peace?

And so he'd have his peace
for the rest of our day.

He'd have it that night, too:
pot scratch, red shells whistling,

at last claw snap, leg crack,
lemon, melted butter—

long days of wiring boats
for not-enough money,

long nightmare nights
of Korean shrapnel

pushed aside as he rose
from his usual hunch

to ask how we liked them
while we stared at our hands,

our plates, the sleeping dogs
beneath the glass table,

at anything but him,
bright-eyed, loose, now, from beer,

who'd leave later that year,
who sucked from his fingers

last bits of crab he'd pulled
peacefully from the sea.

Okay

My father cracks another can
of Schaefer for himself, pushes
a water cup between my hands
and asks *Are you okay, pal?*

slicing the sink's fluorescent light
when he slides into his chair,
the air Pall Mall smoke and silence
after my mother had locked

herself in their room; after, from my bed,
I'd heard their voices rise, heard
her cry his name, my name, then *don't, don't;*
after his punches; after I'd plowed

my head into his gut; after he'd said
I'll understand when I was his age.

                    *

Older now than he was then, I am still
the boy who doesn't understand,

who can't catch his breath across
the glass table, can't speak or stop
shaking, can't sip that water through
the knot in his throat, who still snaps

awake at night, hearing his mother
calling for him beneath his father
in the hallway, in their bedroom,
from the kitchen's linoleum floor,

who will never be okay, never
speak the lie that his father,
even in death, sits, hands folded,
eyes bloodshot, waiting to hear.

Greg's Poem

for Gregory Loper, killed in a hit-and-run
on November 18, 2011, in Philadelphia, PA

and for the neighbors who tackled
the man who killed him when he tried to flee the scene

The scrapper's story ends
    on the sidewalk

at Jasper and Lehigh,
    front rim bent

into an "8,"
    head in a blood puddle.

Ends on his way to a store,
    a few blocks

from his house and his wife
    and his eleven kids

and stepkids, with rubberneckers
    palming their mouths,

with police tape ringing bike
    shrapnel and shattered

glass, ringing the SUV that hurled
    him there, with a squad

car's staccato red/blue/red/blue
    above the cuffed driver

neighbors tackled
    when he tried to run.

*

Ends twenty years earlier, when
      he hears a corner preacher

talking big money in scrap metal—
      appliances and wire,

file cabinets, rusted fans—
      when he starts mapping

trash days, Dumpsters, empty lots,
      a boss for the first time.

Ends when he meets the woman
      who'll make him quit

gangbanging after four shots
      to the thigh could not,

who'll cradle the side mirror
      of the car that killed him

to keep close the last thing
      that touched him alive,

who'll tell reporters she wants to know
      why the driver's DUI

the day before jailed him for just hours,
      why he'd been released

without bail on his own recognizance,
      why he was anywhere near a car,

let alone a road, let alone the bike lane
        her husband stayed perfectly within.

*

The scrapper's story ends
        in that bike lane

on someone's surveillance tape.
        He's peddling left to right

against traffic, no helmet,
        working uphill,

shoulders hunched from lugging
        all that scrap metal,

from, his stepdaughter said,
        carrying his family on his back,

the bike's reflectors gleaming
        in dusk's headlights

as he strides beyond the frame,
        beyond this life.

Old Man Shooting Free Throws

His body tells you he's worked on this routine
    all his life: two hard dribbles
        through baggy sweatpants,
two slow knee bends before he settles into a third,
    eyes closed, head clear of anything
        but this moment in which he lets out
a long, slow breath, mumbles something,
    then sets his feet shoulder-width apart,
        squares those shoulders to the foul line
and baseline, to the half-moon backboard
    cracked in one corner
        before he opens his eyes again
and fixes them just over the rim,
    rusted, netless,
        breathing in exhaust
and road dust as the ball settles
    into the cradle his right fingertips make,
        his bent wrist even with his glasses
before he hops and grunts
    behind a gooseneck follow-through
        and his one-handed shot flies free.

Girl on a Playground Swing

Bored of the turning bars and monkey bars,
　　　the walking bridge and spring rides
　　　　　and see-saw far too tall for her,
she slides her fingers through links
　　　in the swing's metal chains and jumps,
　　　　　pulls up her knees,
plops herself onto the creased rubber seat,
　　　straightening her legs and sandaled toes,
　　　　　smiling beyond the sandbox
and ball field, beyond anyone who is not three,
　　　who did not just, on her own, trade
　　　　　the earth for dreams of rock
and sway, of arcing higher, then higher still,
　　　bending her neck and body back,
　　　　　inviting gravity to somehow
swing her, a supplicant with arms raised,
　　　a pendulum at rest,
　　　　　toward an orbit all her own.

Teaching My Daughter to Ride Her Bike, I Recall the One My Father Stole for Me from a Black Child

On the flat sidewalk
  our four-year-old
stands on her pedals,

pushing and grunting
  but getting nowhere,
and something in how

she cries and looks back
  and tries again
and looks back and how

she screams when her shin
  slams the pedal
and how she falls sideways

and takes the bike with her
  takes me back
to my seventh summer.

My father, home from work,
  calls me from the yard.
Got you a bike, he says,

holding one handlebar
  until I take the other,
which is black like the seat

and the tires and the race
  of the kid from whom
he took it at a stop sign

after third shift.
              You should have seen
how wide his eyes got,

my father tells me, laughing.
              He says *Smell the seat.*
I bet it still smells like nigger.

I bend down like he tells me
              and don't smell anything
but his truck's exhaust

and a neighbor's barbecue,
              but I tell him
Yeah, yeah, it does,

and he smiles,
              heads into the house.
Help me lift my fork

at dinner that night
              when he recounts
how the kid stopped riding

right in the middle of the street
              and my father
couldn't get around,

how my father jumped
              from his truck
and yelled at the kid

and the kid yelled back
              and my father said
What did you just say?

and the kid didn't answer
       so my father asked again
while the kid tried to ride away,

not so tough all of a sudden,
       but couldn't get anywhere,
too weak to pedal uphill—

that kid, who had to be crying
       as my father closed in,
had to be clenching those handlebars

because he didn't want
       to give up his bike or to die
at the hands of a man he feared,

I know, had murder in him.
       I've seen those eyes.
I pulled those hands back

from my mother's neck
       like he pulled that boy's
one by one from that bike

while someone waited for him
       in a park or a school
or a church or a house

like our house, which the bank
       would claim before long.
Before long, my daughter

will ask
       what my father was like,
and, since I can't go back

to my seventh year and lock him
        in his truck, after I tell her
that most nights he read in a chair

by the front window and after
        I tell her about his pompadour
and pocket T-shirts, his Pall Malls,

his cans of Schaefer, his whistle
        when he drove,
his stubble when he kissed me,

I'll tell her I loved him very much
        and I'll begin to tell her
the stories within this story.

My Aunt Edna Gives Me a Postcard Photo

My Aunt Edna wasn't ready.
For sixty years, she's stared

blank-faced past the camera's eye.
My father's arm drapes her shoulder.

She doesn't hug him back,
hands folded in her lap, curtains open,

blinds closed behind them.
It might be evening, after dinner,

high-ball glasses sweating on a table.
It might be Saturday, my father sore

from labor in workweek weather
in a dress shirt far too big for him.

His stare is hard to read:
eyes squinted, mouth a straight line

beside his sister twenty years older
who's now outlived him by twenty years,

whose gives me this photo
when I go to visit after far too long

the only house I can still enter
from my childhood—

same wallpaper mountains,
same end table I crawled under

at three and broke a lamp,
same back porch bench

where she sat with my uncle
and so many others long gone,

where we sit today
and say their names—

her siblings, her daughter,
even her grandchildren now,

the latest a suicide
at rest beneath a pinwheel

in my aunt's garden, which
my aunt looks beyond with a stare

that mirrors her gaze
in the photo I hold in my hands,

her hair combed in the same style,
but gray now, and thin,

her arms and legs so thin
she can no longer stand,

her voice so soft a whisper
I have to kneel beside her,

have to bring my ear to her lips
to hear the last thing

she says before her nurse
tells me she should rest:

I've outlived everyone, Danny.
Everyone. And that's too long.

Birthday Poem for My Mother

If she were alive to read this, my poem
would be different, with her dog in it,

maybe, or grandchildren, or her tomatoes
staked in the four-square-foot plot

behind the row home she raised us in,
with rot holes in the floor big enough

to swallow shoes into the cave
of that dirt cellar, which was always wet,

which seeped like acid into old photos
and washed them clean. And even if

it were happy she would have cried,
not that she would have understood it

or cared to, or wanted it as much
as flowers she could set like a trophy

on the entertainment center, but
because she cried, it seemed, so often.

Birthdays, weddings, old movies
and songs, TV shows, long-lost names…

or an ordinary Tuesday with no wind,
blue skies, a pair of cardinals…

and suddenly her face closed
on itself with how cleanly she'd cut

herself from her family when
they said my father was no good,

and with how my father left her
to fend for herself and for us,

and her unable to, going on welfare,
holding my hand the first of each month

outside the Saint Francis Mission,
where we waited for Father Pat

to bless the free butter and cheese.
She would have shown the poem

to my sister at dinner tonight,
to her neighbors tomorrow,

then stuck it to the refrigerator
to disappear behind coupons.

She would have said it was *beaut-ee-ful*,
like the canal I'm sitting by as I write this,

no matter how ugly it was.
A woman rode by on a bike

earlier with my mother's hair,
freshly permed and cut short,

hair-sprayed in place. She waved
at me and shook her head,

and since then I've been ten again.
It's been midsummer, the sun low

over the Center City skyline.
I've just came in from the hydrant

and my mother is holding open
a towel. How close we get

to the dead sometimes: her knees
crack as she squats. She waves me close.

She smells like spaghetti sauce.
Her fingers are the slipperiness

hot water washes from pasta
as she cloaks me until I'm warm.

The Nun and the Roaches

for Maria Mazziotti Gillan

It was just before Christmas. Eighth grade.
    The morning we brought back to school
        the sales kits of crap

Sister gave us to hawk on Jesus' behalf—
    ceramic crosses, chocolate bars,
        wrapping paper, ribbon spools.

It was the chocolate, I bet, that drew roaches
    to the box, which I'd stashed in a corner
        behind the folding cot

I slept on and forgotten about. If I'd opened it
    even that morning I'd have known,
        but I didn't, and now there they were,

dozens of roaches long as my thumb crawling
    around the box Sister held open
        in that second-floor, cinderblock hall,

asking me *What's this all about?*
        Thirty years later, I want to think
            she was concerned, but

when I wept by the window
        overlooking the El and the railroad
            and the shuttered Y,

no one held me. I should have known
        roaches would find the box because
            they'd found everything else.

Our dirty dishes. Our toothbrushes.
        Our Easter baskets. My mother
            had told me not to tell

anyone our house's truths, that some things
          no one else needs to know.
               After my father left,

I told my friends he worked nights.
          When all we had to eat was cheese
               from the soup kitchen,

I told them grilled cheese was my favorite,
          served them cheese hunks on Saltines
               and bragged that we were rich.

But when Sister said I'd have to pay
          for the kit, when she asked me
               what I thought my father

would say when she called him, I betrayed
          my mother and told her everything:
               He was living with his sister

in Bristol or maybe
          his buddy in Mayfair. He said
               he'd call, but he hadn't.

I told Sister about the glass he'd smashed
          against my mother's cheek,
               the money he took with him

for the exterminator.
          There are mice, too, I said,
               and we hold our back door

shut with a broom handle. I could see already
          my mother sinking in her chair
               in the principal's office,

could see her crying into cupped hands.
But I couldn't see her lying
to the nuns, to the God

we thanked for our lives each bedtime
and for His *gifts* and *bounty*
each evening

when we bowed our heads at the glass table,
a curled yellow fly strip
over the gas stove,

the mice quiet somewhere
until we were in bed,
the roaches

never giving a damn, fearless
or dumb, striding whenever
they wanted

through cracks in the walls,
up our chair and table legs,
across our plates,

flailing their antennae until
we flung them to the floor
and stomped them

or they scurried off
and lay so still we thought
them gone, a shame

we could, after all, keep in our house,
telling ourselves it wasn't unbearable
until someone else said that it was.

Pigeon Man, Grafton Street

Dublin, Ireland

As still as Joyce beneath O'Connell's spire
or Wilde atop his Merrion Square rock,
the man statued on Grafton Street's old Éire—

galoshes to his knees, sparse hair slicked back,
his eyes black stones, his hands perches for birds,
all of them gray against the wet brick walk,

his glare fixed like your pop's through pecks and turds,
through camera clicks and clinks into his tin.
Like your pop did, this busker hoards his words,

won't tell you who he is or where he's been,
won't see you through whatever holds his stare,
will leave tonight just to come back again,

as silent as his grave these twenty years,
as still as Joyce beneath O'Connell's spire.

Poem Ending with a Union Vote

Construction Zone Ahead. The shop foreman
surfs from talk to ballgame to classic rock,
blinker on, stuck in a closing right lane
until Mr. Sunglasses waves him in—

all mirrored shades, gold chains, and half-open
shirt, all smiles until the shop foreman smiles
and waves back in his rearview as red hair
settles on Sunglasses's lowered shoulder.

The foreman mourns pay and benefit cuts
proposed at a management meeting where
he'd spent the better part of an hour
fretting over what to do with his hands.

Cuts to guys he'd worked with twenty years,
drank beer, played softball, built kitchens with, cried.
Guys who knew him better than his ex.
He'd shuffled the crisp stack of attachments,

alphabetized them by the first letter
on each unread page. He'd circled and checked.
He'd scribbled marginal notes and made sure
not to doodle. Then he'd moved to adjourn

so he could return to his apartment
and settle between Scotch burn and himself.
He eyes his mirror until the couple
vanishes behind wiper blur, rainbow,

Sunglasses waving in car after car,
a conductor dissolving into myth,
his lover revising herself, tracing
brows, cheekbones, lips, finger-combing her hair—

a special night ahead for them, maybe,
or big day wrapping up, the two of them
in a zone of slow time and long kisses
while the foreman clicks off his radio,

becomes flares, work cones, now and then a honk,
a jackhammer, a brake flash, a craned neck,
pushing his ear into his cold window,
into the idling engine of his life.

Vanishing

I was twenty, free from money, free from love,
buzzed on skunk weed and skunked beer.
They'd flashed me from a third-floor window, smiling.

We'd joked of this—my neighbor, her friend.
They invited me in.
They met me on creaking hallway stairs.

They took my hands, turned off the only light.
I felt myself moving. I did as I was told.
Among two women, a kind of vanishing.

*

Among two women, a kind of vanishing.
I felt myself moving. I did as I was told.
They took my hands, turned off the only light.

They met me on creaking hallway stairs.
They invited me in.
We'd joked of this—my neighbor, her friend.

They'd flashed me from a third-floor window, smiling,
buzzed on skunk weed and skunked beer.
I was twenty, free from money, free from love.

Making Shepherd's Pie on St. Patty's Day
While My Neighbors Have Make-Up Sex

My neighbor Mike is a lowlife ass hat,
        a drunken douche clown
with a dipshit dog and a pencil for a penis—

or at least that's what
        his girlfriend Sue proclaimed
this afternoon while I peeled parsnips

and carrots, chopped celery root
        and garlic and onions,
while I hummed "Danny Boy"

and "Galway Girl" on my side
        of our shared kitchen wall,
only half-tuned to their fight

until something shattered over there
        and his dog yelped
and Sue shouted—screamed,

really, shredding her throat—
        that they were through.
The keys to Shepherd's Pie

are the potatoes and the lamb,
        first thrown together
long ago in a stone cottage

by some frugal farmer's wife.
        I don't know where
Mike and Sue got thrown together,

but I've got twenty bucks
   that says it wasn't church,
no matter how enthusiastically

Sue used the Lord's name
   after she and Mike made up,
no matter how angelic her falsetto,

how pitch-perfect her vibrato
   over Mike's garbage disposal,
Mike's wobbly kitchen table,

and against the thin wall dividing us,
   where Sue got absolutely
evangelical before halting mid-word

like she'd just noticed she was lost,
   then finding herself,
her breath, her voice again, louder now,

then louder still, chant-singing
   in a tongue reserved
for the damned and the saved

while my lamb filling blended
   rosemary and sage, thyme,
Worcestershire sauce,

while my potatoes lay boiled
   and bored and some part
of Sue or Mike thunked Sheetrock

with the insistence and metronomic
            precision of a choir conductor
or of any good shepherd

committed to setting the last
            stubborn post in a fence
no matter how hard the wind blew

or how threatening the sky became,
            no matter how loudly
his neighbor, simmering, complained.

Third Month

She slips into deep sleeps
in the afternoon now.
Stripped to panties and bra,
she curls into the posture
the new one will take
inside her this month,
the size of a small peach.
She pulls the blanket
to her neck and dreams
it is summer, sunlight
through every window,
room filled with ginger
and purple trumpets.
She passes him the baby
and they sing together.
They have waited so long,
the moment breaks them,
but they do not stop their song.
It happens while she sleeps:
nubs becoming fingers and toes,
black spots, eyes,
the room shifting into balance
around her easy breaths.
The new one swimming closer
to their arms.

Ice Skating with Abigail

Again this year you and I
lace rentals and wobble
until we find our strides

and glide from the boards
to the center of the ice,
where you, at scvcn, weave

us through couples and kids,
around orange cones,
80s music loud now

that we've stopped
talking of fear and falling
and are simply going,

our breath steaming
past the hot cocoa stand
and our locker stuffed with shoes

on this day so close
to my parents' death dates
I could leave here

and sit again in the stillness
of their last rooms, conjure
the miracle of their chests

rising and falling, hold
their cold hands, hear
them whisper *love* to me

or scratch it on a napkin
and yet still be here with you
as our blades scratch

around the rink until
we're the only ones left
in a moment that you'll forget,

most likely, ever happened,
us chopping and striding,
making our marks while we can.

At the Commercial Audition

The white door opens and another
    four kids spill
        into the hushed hall,

falling into each other, laughing,
    just as wired as they were
        in the audition room

where they wrestled for the remote,
    where they feigned to care
        who won or lost a game

that happened only in their heads
    and the head of the director,
        who's been tasked

with finding a quartet of young actors
    good enough to make us buy
        that they're best friends,

to make you and me
    believe that our lives
        will never be as full

or happy as theirs without
    more cable channels
        and movies on demand,

without agreeing to additional,
    mysterious surcharges
        that no one here

knows or cares anything about
    as the crew adjusts
        mics and lights

and the four kids gather
        their jackets and binders
                and the flawless

photos of their faces
        while a thirteen-year-old
                in a blue blouse

that brings out her eyes
        crosses her new shoes,
                watches the wall clock,

stares into the backs of her hands
        beside her father,
                who'd pulled her

from school when, for the first time
        in months, her manager
                waved before them

the carrot of a three-minute audition
        three hours away
                if they could get there,

and here they are, shoulder-to-shoulder
        as they'd been on the rattling train
                before the door opens

and the woman with the clipboard
        calls out a name that makes
                the girl and her father look up.

The Background Noise I've Heard All My Life

A woodpecker won't stop hammering
my house, *tap-tap, tap-tap-tap,*

and just when I think he's done,
he starts again, *tap-tap, tap-tap-tap,*

so all morning I've been going out
to caw like a crow, to wave my arms

thirty feet below where he deepens
and widens the hole he's made,

tap-tap, tap-tap-tap, tap-tap, tap-tap-tap,
and I start to dream of his demise

as the noise I grew up around
on that El-shadowed Philly avenue

comes back—sirens, clacking
trains, bass thump, shattered glass,

cars idling and roaring past,
shouts from growing crowds

when fights spilled out of Tinney's Bar
while I lay in my bed inside movies

and books, fearing what waited for me
in that world I wasn't fit for,

my father long gone,
my mother and sister calling me,

at twelve, *the man of the house*
when all I wanted was to be anyone,

anywhere else. I had no idea, though,
who or where, since every man

I'd known stayed put or got killed
or sped off and never returned

or went to jail and came back
harder and more distant,

the trips our people took confined to
bottles of Jack, cans of Bud

and paint thinner, to sidewalk
folding chairs on summer nights,

maybe a cousin to visit in Jersey,
maybe a weekend down the shore

before another stretch of loading
and welding and pouring and guarding

before coming home to blaring
and screeching and yelling at all hours,

to the cacophony of background noises
I heard my first thirty years, that I hear still,

all those Philly childhood nights
screaming, smashing, clacking, crying

up avenues and interstates, through
toll booths, up train tracks and turnpikes

to swirl among the white birches
behind my house and in this silence

I never imagined myself within,
silence I breathe in every morning

and hold, silence this woodpecker,
oblivious, starving, confused if he's

looking for a matc so late in the year,
can only for a moment disturb.

Nothing, October

You were here weeks fewer
than we thought you were,

but you were here
as surely as we are,

in our small house far from town,
with all we'd hoped for you

coming back this fall morning
that promises snow.

Finished growing at the length
of a girl's thumb, you did not,

unlike your older sister,
shake your mother awake

from the start of things.
Nor did you stir those nights

I sang into her belly:
the first sign we ignored.

Then the easy eight weeks—
no sickness, no wave of weight.

In the doctor's office that afternoon
we were ready only for what

we'd known: measurements,
a ballpark due date,

the churning engine of your heart.
But you were as thin and still as a pen.

After the medicine and the cramps,
after the year of blood tests

that said your mother was
still pregnant, we had only

your half-painted room
and a stand of slumping

white birches beneath
a smoke-gray October sky.

It's two years later,
October again.

Wet brown leaves slick
our steps and blacktop.

This morning, baby Eliza
looked up from her crib

and said *Hi* to the wall,
her mobile, then me,

squinting as she smiled,
kicked, and stretched,

her eyes beautiful blue
as yours would have been.

The chimney sweep's
coming today. I'm chopping

celery and onions
for chowder and speaking

again to that place in me,
that pocket of air where you live.

In Praise of Lying Flat on My Back

after a photograph by Gail Goepfert

How rare it is
that I'm like this
beyond the seconds
it takes to fall
into bed and roll
to my right side,

how sensuous
to lie among yarrow
and purple salvias
and prostrate myself
to a noon sun
that blows into me
a breath I squeeze
in my core
before I hush it out
through my teeth

and to the wind
that touches me
wherever it wants
because I need it
to touch me today

as I lie so still
in my garden
my neighbors might
think me dead
as my grandfather
who kicked off
at my age

but I'm not headed
anywhere I know of
except a meeting

I'd rather skip
and I am not at all
ready to die

and yes soon I'll rise
to modified foods
and terror and no jobs
for my daughters

and will cruise
with windows down
to a windowless room
and nod and vote
and stare into my hands
until someone asks
for a motion to adjourn

but that is not now.

Now, for once,
I will take my time.
I will lie flat on my back
in this moment
inside which a woodpecker
taps long as a phone ring,
again and again,
into my neighbor's oaks

inside which yellowthroats
and redstarts warble
high in our white birches

inside which, as I rest
on compost and mulch
and feel myself here
and see myself gone

and watch the stems
of these two Sulfur Cosmos
bend toward the sun,

I want to be so much
more than afraid.

Testament

in memory of Victoria Leigh Soto,
a first-grade teacher at Sandy Hook Elementary School
who died shielding her students
in Newtown, CT, on December 14, 2012

Because her Aunt Debbie
      was a teacher, so was Vicki,
            who put in ten- and twelve-

hour days plus weekends and summers
      for her students, her *angels,*
            Vicki's aunt's hands moving

with her hands, her aunt's
      voice pitched to her own
            in that first-grade classroom

alive with light, Vicki's life
      a testament to her aunt's,
            her author's teas and parent

conferences, her class's PJ Days
      and gingerbread houses a debt
            paid forward, a story continued,

Vicki's Morning Meetings,
      where she'd hear her angels' stories
            and share her own,

where she'd read
      while they sat on mats at her feet—
            crisscross apple sauce,

saddled on their shoes, laughing,
      shifting—are also testaments,
            Ms. Soto's stories unfolding

one glossed page after another,
        her voice the room's center,
                Ms. Soto's stories spilling later

through gapped smiles
        across dinner tables,
                at bath time and bed time,

across back seats on drives
        to school, the dentist, the shore.
                Ms. Soto's stories, Vicki's stories:

testaments inscribed, now,
        in the air that surrounds us,
                where words cannot hold

how Vicki counted herself
        as nothing that morning
                and, stepping in front

of the gunman, gave herself,
        gave to her angels who survived
                and her angels who fell with her

a testament
        to love beyond measure,
                beyond the book of time.

Self-Portrait at the Block Party

By nine a.m., my old block
      is beach umbrellas
and pennant banners,

ashtrays, iced coolers,
      arcs of nylon folding chairs.
Bad Company blares

from a boom box. Brian
      from our grade school
wails on spatula-guitar

through "Shooting Star"
      and "Can't Get Enough,"
eyes squeezed, mouth wide

to June's harmonic sky,
      same look
I saw so many Saturday nights

half our lives ago—
      still the crew cut,
the Fighting Leprechaun tattoo

closed-fisted on his shoulder
      above two smoldering
hibachis, where his grilled

breakfast smokes the city air,
      pork roll and scrapple,
eggs scrambled in a pan,

toast popping up in a window
      propped open above
card tables, beer kegs,

kids splashing in plastic pools,
        above sidewalk-
chalked tigers and pines and

an inflatable slide yet to rise,
        above the makeshift stage
where, later, spirits I thought

long gone will rise, too—
        Fonzie back on vocals,
Tiny set up behind drums.

The old guys,
        we called them,
long-haired and bearded

those first years after 'Nam,
        old guys
fresh out of high school

with us just starting third or
        fourth grade,
and now here we are: old guys,

old women, or getting there,
        sipping lager
over sopping paper plates,

a little drunk by the time
        the band starts, a little high,
not much left to say

except we knew each other
        once upon a time
in white T-shirts

and black fingerless gloves
       and in the back
seats of borrowed cars,

when tight city blocks
       like this one opened
to highways that outlasted

nights our parents
       yelled back and forth
until one of them swung,

highways that took us
       to the shore,
the Poconos, the Maryland line,

highways dark and limitless,
       calling to us
even as Timmy's old Charger

cooled outside the Aramingo Diner
       after we'd driven all night
to nowhere and back, first purple

over the skyline, papers not yet
       on doorsteps, highways
on which we screamed the songs

that were our poetry,
       songs *the old guys*
at last start into: "Roxanne,"

"Heart of Gold," "Lola,"
       "Thunder Road."
Then Fonzie tells us to raise a glass

for our lost ones, and I hold
        in my mind the way
sun fell on their faces—

my parents, my overdosed cousins,
        my friend Jake gone early
from a stroke, Gina J. stabbed

beneath an underpass, Wild C,
        who was like a brother,
jumping in front of an El train.

I hear their laughs again, the way each
        said my name.
I feel myself inside of their arms,

feel their silence swell in me
        until everyone starts sipping
in memorium,

the whole block tilted red cups
        in right hands. I catch
myself in a storm door window

blurry enough to be a guy
        about to settle on his stoop
and sing along, nodding, elbows

on knees because he belongs,
        or a guy about to disappear
beyond the soup kitchen

and the shuttered bank
        and the Starlite Ballroom,
now a rehab, where this band

once rocked for hours.
        One of us swallows
the lager's last burn.

The other is already gone.

Bike Ride

"Rails to Trails" Bolton Notch Bike Trail, Bolton, CT

Down the trail we ride, my daughter and I,
dodging dog walkers and joggers, pumping

stride for stride over crushed gravel and mud,
once in a while a sepia photo

rising from the bulldozed '20s to show
us where things stood: *ticket booth, train station,*

in almost every shot a man donning
a Stetson, seated, alone, bowed forward like

my father over our kitchen table
in the dark, lost to Schaefer's, Pall Malls, bills,

lost now to the ground almost twenty years,
though I still see him mouthing our shared name,

still feel his stubbled cheek on mine when time
grew short, and still I feel his calloused palms

in the small of my back that summer night
just dark enough for fireflies and porch lights,

when he swiped the kickstand and led me down
our drive, a 10-hour shift of wiring boats

just done, another, or a longer one
waiting while he ran beside me as far

as he could, then pushed me off, leading me
toward his death and my mother's, toward

four jobs in three states, no place ever home
after that first home, leading me somehow

to eastern Connecticut and this trail,
where my daughter pulls past, smiling, puffing

hard, taller now than her mom, calling me
to race her in the falling August light.

The New York Quarterly Foundation, Inc.

New York, New York

Poetry
Magazine

Since 1969

Edgy, fresh, groundbreaking, eclectic—voices from all walks of life.

Definitely NOT your mama's poetry magazine!

The *New York Quarterly* has been defining the term contemporary American poetry since its first craft interview with W. H. Auden.

Interviews • Essays • and of course, lots of poems.

www.nyq.org

No contest! That's correct, NYQ Books are NO CONTEST to other small presses because we do not support ourselves through contests. Our books are carefully selected by invitation only, so you know that NYQ Books are produced with the same editorial integrity as the magazine that has brought you the most eclectic contemporary American poetry since 1969.

Books

www.nyq.org

poetry at the edge™